The City of David

DISCOVERIES FROM THE EXCAVATIONS

Roberta Blender Maltese, Editor

Lisa Tremper Barnes, Director
Philip and Muriel Berman Museum of Art at Ursinus College

March 8 - June 30, 1991
Philip and Muriel Berman Museum of Art at Ursinus College

CHRONOLOGICAL TABLE

B.C.E. = Before the Common Era   C.E. = Common Era

The strata (layers) in the City of David and corresponding periods:

STRATUM	PERIOD	
21	Chalcolithic	Second half of 4th millennium B.C.E.
20		
19	Early Bronze	31st - 22nd centuries B.C.E.
18		
17	Middle Bronze II	18th - 16th centuries B.C.E.
16	Late Bronze	14th - 13th centuries B.C.E.
15	Iron I	12th - 11th centuries B.C.E.
14	Iron II	10th century B.C.E.
13	Iron II	9th century B.C.E.
12	Iron II	8th century B.C.E.
11	Iron II	7th century B.C.E.
10	Iron II	End of 7th century B.C.E. - 586 B.C.E.
9	Persian	6th - 4th centuries B.C.E.
8	Early Hellenistic	4th - 2nd centuries B.C.E.
7	Hellenistic (Hasmonean)	Second half of 2nd century B.C.E. - 37 B.C.E.
6	Early Roman (Herodian)	37 B.C.E. - 70 C.E.

CONTENTS

THE CITY OF DAVID: DISCOVERIES FROM THE EXCAVATIONS

EXHIBITION ITINERARY

Philip and Muriel Berman Museum of Art at Ursinus College
Collegeville, Pa.
March 8 - June 30, 1991

Lehigh University Art Galleries, Lehigh University
Bethlehem, Pa.
September 6 - October 17, 1991

The Harvard Semitic Museum, Harvard University
Cambridge, Mass.
October 31, 1991 - January 3, 1992

Cobb Institute of Archaeology
Mississippi State, Miss.
January 22 - May 30, 1992

The Skirball Museum, Hebrew Union College
Los Angeles, Calif.
January - March 1993

Exhibition on loan from the Institute of Archaeology, Hebrew University
of Jerusalem, Israel

Exhibition circulated by the Philip and Muriel Berman Museum of Art at
Ursinus College

ACKNOWLEDGMENTS

It is with great pride that the Philip and Muriel Berman Museum of Art at Ursinus College hosts the inaugural exhibition in the United States of *The City of David: Discoveries from the Excavations*.

It is rare for an art museum to have the opportunity to arrange the loan of artifacts from an archaeological excavation. While professional archaeologists, historians, and the thousands of people who volunteer at digs in Israel have access to such concentrated evidence of ancient cultures, it is unusual for the general public to have the chance to view them so comprehensively. This exhibition was developed by the Institute of Archaeology of the Hebrew University of Jerusalem. It focuses on the long history of the City of David as revealed through eight years of excavation, from 1978-1985, just outside the walls of the Old City of Jerusalem.

In Jerusalem, the exhibition attracted many visitors, including Muriel and Philip Berman, who brought it to my attention. In it, the viewer vicariously experiences the excavation through a sampling of artifacts, photographs, and drawings.

With the cooperation of the Institute of Archaeology and the Israel Antiquities Authority, the Berman Museum of Art has arranged for the material not only to travel to our institution, but to tour nationally. The exhibition will also be seen at the Lehigh University Art Galleries, The Harvard Semitic Museum, the Cobb Institute of Archaeology, and The Skirball Museum, Hebrew Union College.

The City of David: Discoveries from the Excavations was curated by Gila Hurvitz, director of exhibitions at the Institute of Archaeology. Thanks are extended to Gila for her assistance in organizing this loan and to Ruta Peled, Israel Antiquities Authority, and Yoram Tsafrir, director of the Institute of Archaeology, for their endorsement of this unique collaboration.

Nancy E. Francis, collections manager of the Berman Museum of Art and our cadre of student assistants continue to ensure that our operation runs smoothly, and I thank them for their efforts. Roberta B. Maltese, catalogue editor, symposium participant, and City of David excavation volunteer, provided invaluable assistance in preparing our presentation of this exhibition, and I am grateful for her participation. Finally, I thank Muriel and Philip Berman for planting the seed of opportunity and for encouraging us to broaden our horizons in providing for a multitude of cultural experiences.

Lisa Tremper Barnes, Director, Philip and Muriel Berman Museum of Art at Ursinus College.

CONTRIBUTORS

Gila Hurvitz is the director of exhibitions at the Institute of Archaeology, Hebrew University of Jerusalem, and the curator of *The City of David: Discoveries from the Excavations.*

Dr. Robert L. Cohn is associate professor of religion and the Philip and Muriel Berman Scholar in Jewish Studies at Lafayette College in Easton, Pa. He is the author of *The Shape of Sacred Space: Four Biblical Studies* (1981) and coauthor of *Exploring the Hebrew Bible* (1988). He has written numerous articles on biblical narrative, most recently "From Homeland to Holy Land: The Territoriality of Torah," *Continuum* 1: (1990).

Hershel Shanks is the founder, editor, and publisher of *Biblical Archeology Review* and *Bible Review.* He is also the editor and publisher of *Moment* magazine.

Roberta B. Maltese is a textbook editor with a special interest in archaeology in Israel. She has worked in Jerusalem with Israeli archaeologists publishing their research in English and was editor of the catalogue for the exhibition *King Herod's Dream: Caesarea by the Sea.* Ms. Maltese participated in the excavations in the City of David (five seasons), at Rehovot-in-the-Negev, and at Caesarea.

Technical consultants to the editor: David Tarler and Jane M. Cahill, former supervisors, City of David, Area G.

February 14, 1991
30 Shevat 5751

Dear Friends of Ursinus' Berman Museum of Art:

It is a great honor to bring greetings to you from the State of Israel in hosting *The City of David: Discoveries from the Excavations* archaeological exhibition, which is making its American debut at the Berman Museum of Art at Ursinus College.

Jerusalem is a city suspended between heaven and earth. Its towers stretch upward from the hilltops to the skies; its ancient stones reach down to the bedrock in which it is rooted.

The exhibition at the Berman Museum of Art presents discoveries made in the archaeological excavation at the ancient City of David. Layers and layers of past eras in Jerusalem have been uncovered, bearing out history and tradition. It is an historic opportunity for people to view artifacts who may never have an opportunity to visit Israel and see them at their original site.

I hope those who view this cultural and educational adventure will make new discoveries of their own.

With best wishes for a resoundingly successful event,

Sincerely yours,

Israel Peleg, Ph.D.
Consul General of Israel
Philadelphia

FOREWORD

When Yigal Shiloh began work in the City of David, he was the latest in a long series of scholars who had struggled to unveil the secrets of that long, rather narrow hill. Once the discovery was made in the late 19th century that the southeastern hill of Jerusalem was in fact the site of the capital of the United Kingdom and of Judah, it became a magnet for researchers and excavators. Among those researchers we find many of the great names in archaeology: Weill, Macalister and Duncan, Crowfoot and Fitzgerald, and Kenyon. The City of David Project was, however, the largest and most comprehensive excavation on the site.

It was difficult to find a large undisturbed area to excavate. Yigal had to use all of his diplomatic gifts in renting land for excavation from local Arab landowners. Subsequently, he had to draw on all his courage in opposing Orthodox Jewish extremists who condemned him for excavating an area they believed had been a cemetery. The burdens of administration and external disturbances did not overshadow the real challenge, however: to carry out an extensive and meticulous excavation using modern methods and techniques. Yigal and his team have indeed retrieved an enormous amount of new data for studying Jerusalem and Judah in the biblical period. All his efforts in his last years and during his illness were dedicated to research and publication of the results of the excavations at the City of David and its finds.

Yigal Shiloh did not live to see this exhibition, one of the fruits of his devotion to the City of David. It opened in the exhibition hall at the Institute of Archaeology of the Hebrew University of Jerusalem on the second anniversary of his death. He died on November 14, 1987, at the age of 50.

The excavations in the City of David were part of the extensive activity of the Institute of Archaeology at the sites of ancient Jerusalem. They followed the large-scale excavations near the Temple Mount, directed by B. Mazar, and the excavations in the Jewish Quarter, directed by N. Avigad. These two founding fathers of the archaeology of Israel, together with the late Y. Yadin and M. Avi-Yonah, were the most prominent of Yigal Shiloh's teachers—and those of many of us, his friends, the "second generation" of Israeli archaeologists.

The Institute of Archaeology was a second home to Yigal Shiloh. He was born in Haifa in 1937 and after completing his high school education and military service, he began his studies in archaeology and Jewish history in Jerusalem. He received his B.A. and M.A. degrees from the Hebrew University, both *summa cum laude*, and in 1974 submitted his Ph.D. dissertation on foreign influences on the masonry of Palestine in the Iron Age. In 1983, already an associate professor, he was elected head of the Institute, in which capacity he served until 1986.

Jerusalem and biblical archaeology are the main areas of Yigal Shiloh's scholarly contribution. His interim report on the City of David excavations appeared in 1984 as volume 19 in the *Qedem* series of monographs published in Jerusalem by the Institute of Archaeology. The series of scientific reports now being prepared, the restoration of Area G in the City of David, and this exhibition are expressions of the excavation's achievements and are a fitting memorial to Yigal Shiloh.

The City of David exhibition is the first our Institute has opened to the public. We thank the City of David Society, especially Mr. Mendel Kaplan, who initiated it; the City of David excavation team; the administration of the Hebrew University; the Israel Antiquities Authority; Philip and Muriel Berman, who enabled the transfer of the exhibition to the United States; and the staff members of the Institute of Archaeology, who devoted much time and effort to mount the exhibition.

The Institute of Archaeology is the oldest and largest university department of archaeology in Israel. It has educated many scholars and students from Israel and abroad and is a key institution in archaeological life and activities. It is our hope that this new venture in displaying our work to the public will be an appropriate and successful means of promoting interest, scholarship, and research in the history and cultures of Israel.

Yoram Tsafrir
Head, Institute of Archaeology
Hebrew University of Jerusalem

INTRODUCTION

THE CITY OF DAVID: DISCOVERIES FROM THE EXCAVATIONS

The excavation of the City of David was directed by the late Yigal Shiloh on behalf of the City of David Society. The Society's founders included the Institute of Archaeology of the Hebrew University of Jerusalem, the Israel Exploration Society, the Jerusalem Foundation, and a group of South African sponsors headed by Mr. Mendel Kaplan. The excavations uncovered chapters in the history of Jerusalem from the Chalcolithic period up to and including the Muslim period. The exhibition concentrates on discoveries from the inception of settlement on the eastern hill in the Early Bronze Age to the destruction of Jerusalem in 70 C.E.

1. Early Bronze Age house with benches along its walls, ascribed to ca. 3100 B.C.E.

Bronze Age Jerusalem

Architectural remains demonstrate an Early Bronze Age I settlement. In the excavation's Area E, two dwellings built on bedrock were discovered. They have benches built along their inside walls and are similar to the "broadhouse" common at various Early Bronze Age sites in the country.
[1, 2]

The city wall is the major find from the Middle Bronze Age II period. Structures, floors, and pottery, which are related to the inside of the wall, date its construction to the 18th century B.C.E.
[3, 4]

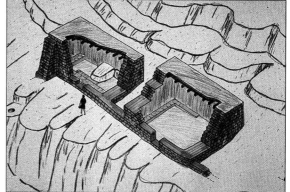

2. Isometric reconstruction of two Early Bronze Age houses.

3. Aerial view, Area E. Bronze Age city wall reused in the Iron Age.

4. Foreground: Segment of Middle Bronze Age city wall built on bedrock. Above it are remains of structures built on a system of stepped terraces in the 8th–7th centuries B.C.E. Top: Terrace wall attributed to the 2nd century B.C.E.–1st century C.E.

During the Late Bronze Age, a dense system of foundation walls was erected below the summit of the southeastern slope, running both north to south and east to west, to create "boxes" containing stone fill. This construction protruded beyond the natural topographical contours, resulting in an addition to the building area of some 250 square meters. The leveled and stepped construction apparently served as a base for the Canaanite citadel and acropolis of Jerusalem during the Late Bronze Age. [5]

5. Aerial view, Area G, looking west. Note that the Iron Age remains are on top of the stepped-stone structure.

Iron Age Jerusalem

The transformation of Jebusite Jerusalem into the capital of the United Kingdom in the 10th century B.C.E. is evident in the city's plan in Stratum 14. The builders of the new capital preserved the Canaanite city plan (the lower city and the citadel) and added the area of the Temple Mount to the north.

In this period of Jerusalem's history, the city's first water system, known as Warren's Shaft, was built. [See Photo 21.] It is similar in construction to water-supply systems in other Israelite royal centers in the 10th-9th centuries B.C.E. Among the outstanding finds of that period are a fragment of a ritual stand and a fist from a bronze statuette. [6,7]

6. Fist from a bronze statuette, 10th century B.C.E.

7. Relief fragment from a terra cotta ritual stand, 10th century B.C.E.

In Stratum 12, dated to the 8th century B.C.E., the city wall on the eastern slope was uncovered for a length of about 120 meters. The wall had been reconstructed and widened, using the Middle Bronze Age wall as a core. The city wall here also served as a retaining wall for the system of terraces constructed on the slope above it. [See Photo 4.]

Pottery figurines are a characteristic find from the Iron Age. The corpus of approximately 1,500 figurines from the City of David is not only extremely varied, but it is also the largest found in Israel. Remains of white slip and paint can be discerned on many of them. Most are handmade; only a few were made in a mold. The figurines can be classified into three groups: human figures, animals, and furniture. [8]

8. Iron Age pottery figurines.

The "House of Ahiel" is a large four-room house, in the southern part of the excavation's Area G, one of several Israelite structures discovered. Two ostraca [sherds used as "scratch paper"] bearing the name "Ahiel," found inside and nearby this structure, have given the house its name. [9] Various service rooms and storerooms adjoined the house, in one of which 37 storage jars were found. [10] It is possible that the inscribed ashlar found in the debris surrounding the house was once affixed to one of the walls. [11]

The Babylonian Destruction

The final stage in the history of the kingdom of Judah is reflected in the archaeological remains of five dwellings that met their end when Jerusalem was destroyed in 586 B.C.E. The signs of ruin and conflagration are evidence of the total destruction of the city. The destruction layers sealed a large quantity of finds of different kinds, which enable an understanding of the essence and character of various aspects of the material culture of Jerusalem in that period. [12]

9. One of the ostraca inscribed with the name "Ahiel."

Together with domestic utensils, kitchenware, and varied epigraphic material, two types of arrowheads were found: the flat iron arrowheads typical of the Israelite period and bronze arrowheads with three ribs and a shaft, known as Scythian, that were used by foreign armies. These remains of fire and warfare are the result of the Babylonian king Nebuchadnezzar's siege of Jerusalem in 586.

The Bullae

In the "House of Bullae," which was excavated along a narrow strip on the eastern border of Area G, 51 small lumps of clay were discovered that had sealed documents and letters.[See Photo 25.] They form the largest group of Hebrew seals with clearly legible impressions found in a stratigraphic context. The bullae were concentrated in one corner on the floor of the house, amid a quantity of ash. The conflagration of the stratum baked the bullae, thereby ensuring their excellent state of preservation. Two unusually shaped vessels also found in the house are large kraters with trumpet bases, with excellent slip and wheel burnish. Of special interest are four objects of soft limestone, which apparently served as ritual stands. [13]

10. From a service room adjacent to Ahiel's house: a stone toilet seat, the thick plaster floor in which it was set, and a ceramic bowl found next to it. Analysis of the soil from the cesspit has shown that ancient Jerusalemites suffered from at least three different intestinal parasites.

The Persian Period

The City of David excavations uncovered a large group of impressions of official seals of the Persian period. These seal impressions, which generally appear on handles of storage jars and only rarely on the bodies of vessels, were probably made by officials for purposes of taxation. Some of the seal impressions bear the name of the province and the name and title of the governor, such as "yhwd/yhw'zr/phw'." Another group of seal

11. Inscribed ashlar from Ahiel's house.

impressions has depictions of lions and includes motifs in the Achaemenid [Persian] style. It is generally accepted that these seals belonged to administrative officials in the province of Judea.

Hellenistic Jerusalem

The extensive building activity in the Hasmonean period is connected with the construction of Jerusalem's "First Wall." According to the first-century Jewish historian Josephus Flavius, this was the first of Jerusalem's three city walls. In the City of David excavations, the wall is part of a stratigraphic sequence, and it is ascribed to the Hasmonean period. Numismatic finds include Ptolemaic, Seleucid, and Hasmonean coins. Among them are coins of Alexander Jannaeus bearing the inscriptions "Yehonatan the King" and "Yehonatan the High Priest and the Council of the Jews." Also found were coins of Yohanan Hyrcanus and Mattathias Antigonus.

Herodian Jerusalem

The destruction of the Second Temple in 70 C.E., at the end of the Great Rebellion against the Romans, is evidenced by signs of a fierce fire and total destruction. In this stratum, a great variety of pottery vessels was found, composed of pottery types in use during the period from the second half of the 1st century B.C.E. to 70 C.E.

A rare find is the lower part of a bone flute, which was never completed. The flute is dated to the time of the siege and destruction. Other finds were the typical stone vessels of Jerusalem, coins of the Roman procurators of the years 11-26 C.E., and a coin from Year Two of the Rebellion, 68 C.E.

Gila Hurvitz

12. Objects __in situ__ in the ash and debris in the bullae room, Area G: (R.–L.) ceramic pot stand, cylindrical "decanter" juglet, and two limestone objects tentatively identified as cultic stands.

13. Assemblage from the bullae room.

Jerusalem As Sacred Center

When David captured the Jebusite stronghold of Jerusalem and made it his personal possession, the "city of David" [II Samuel 5:7-9], he launched Jerusalem toward a special destiny. Militarily, he eliminated a foreign enclave in the midst of Israelite territory. Politically, he created a "federal" capital located between north and south, yet not part of any tribal inheritance. Spiritually, his conquest was to have the most lasting effect. For when David's son Solomon expanded the city of David northward and built there a sanctuary for the worship of YHWH, the god of Israel, he established a sacred center that would come to transcend the geophysical reality of the city. In their descriptions of Jerusalem, biblical and postbiblical writers expressed how they felt themselves to be related to the god who was believed to dwell uniquely in the city. As their political circumstances changed, so did the significance of Jerusalem in the religious imagination.[1] Jerusalem functioned as sacred center in three different senses.

Sacred Mountain

The psalmists and prophets of the Hebrew Bible celebrated Jerusalem as the *axis mundi*, the link between heaven and earth. There YHWH dwelled alongside his chosen king, the descendant of David, and reigned over his land and people. There the priests offered sacrifices whose aromas wafted upward to heaven; there oracles brought down the divine word. This vertical sense of center was encapsulated in the most common biblical epithets for Jerusalem: *har haqqodesh* ("holy mountain") and *har tsion* ("Mount Zion").

Why should Jerusalem have been symbolized as a mountain? The hilltop fortress of the original city of David and the adjoining hill on which the temple was built provided a topographical basis for the designation, yet both are lower than the Mount of Olives flanking them. More importantly, because gods in the ancient Near East frequently were regarded as mountain dwellers, biblical writers were likely using a common literary convention to designate the earthly residence of their god. By celebrating YHWH's reign on Mount Zion, biblical poets proclaimed his hegemony over the land once dominated by the Canaanite god Baal, who dwelled on Mount Zaphon in the north. In addition, when they praised the height, security, and fertility of Mount Zion (e.g., Psalms 48:3; 46:5-6; 65), they were simply transferring to the sacred mountain those positive qualities they associated with the central hill country of their homeland.[2] As sacred mountain, Jerusalem absorbed the features of the real mountains.

Metropolis and *Omphalos*

When Jerusalem was destroyed by the Babylonians in 586 B.C.E., the sacred mountain toppled; the *axis mundi* had been severed. Jews in exile in Babylon could no longer sing the Lord's song (Psalm 137). Though only 50 years later Jerusalem was resettled by returning Jews and the house of YHWH was soon rebuilt, the sacred mountain imagery no longer expressed what Jews experienced Jerusalem to be. As subjects of the Persian emperor, Jews in Jerusalem dwelled precariously in their own land, while those Jews who never returned from exile looked toward Jerusalem from afar. Under these circumstances, Jerusalem was increasingly seen as a horizontal center, a geographic midpoint. From exile in Babylon, one writer envisioned the ransom of scattered Israel from the four cardinal directions and from "the ends of the earth" [Isaiah 43:5]. Eventually, the great pilgrimage festivals brought Jews to Jerusalem from foreign lands, and prayer recited when facing Jerusalem was believed to be especially efficacious [Daniel 6:10; cf. 1 Kings 8:44, 48]. The horizontal connection of the holy temple transcended distance.

As the Persians gave way to the Greeks and they to the Romans, the Jewish diaspora grew. Philo Judaeus (20 B.C.E. - 50 C.E.), a prominent Jew in Alexandria, crystallized the new relationship of these far-flung Jews to Jerusalem in the symbol of the *metropolis*, or mother city. Whatever their places of birth, all Jews, Philo claims, are born spiritually in Jerusalem, their source and foundation (*The Embassy to Gaius*). Thus, although Jews may have many fatherlands, they have but one mother city. What is more, Jerusalem to Jews became what Delphi was to Greeks: *omphalos*, or navel of the earth. Despite its actual geographical coordinates, writers such as Philo and Josephus depicted Jerusalem in the center, or navel, of the land.[3] In the Greco-Roman world, Jews adopted these Greek terms to express their link to a city that provided spiritual nourishment as an antidote to the potential disorder of diaspora.

Past and Future

If biblical writers focused on Zion the sacred mountain and Hellenistic thinkers understood Jerusalem as the *omphalos* of Judea and the metropolis of diaspora Jewry, what was to happen when temple and city were again destroyed? When the Romans put down the Jewish revolt in 70 C.E., they leveled the Second Temple, the symbol of the reconciliation between YHWH and Israel after the Babylonian exile. Now Jerusalem ceased to be a Jewish city; now diaspora was left centerless. The rabbis who reconstituted the Jewish community after the destruction gave expression to an ambivalent attitude toward the sacred center.

On the one hand, the rabbis mourned the Temple's destruction in writing and ritual and prayed for its rebuilding. They were preoccupied with codifying the sacrificial ritual for the day in which they could reinstitute it in a new temple. Jerusalem was the center of the past and its restoration the most fervent desire for the future.

But for the present, on the other hand, life went on without the sacred center. The *omphalos* of Zion was shattered, and Torah (teaching) came forth from the synagogue and the school. Now not the city walls but the "fence around the Torah" provided Jews with a sure defense. In other words, pious attachment to Jerusalem coexisted with a mode of life for which the sacred center functioned only as memory and as hope.

Though primarily diasporic, Jews could not cut their link to the city David founded. That link, which has perdured until the present, explains the inherent fascination with the discovery of the city's earliest past.

Robert L. Cohn

[1.] For a fuller discussion, see R. L. Cohn, *The Shape of Sacred Space: Four Biblical Studies* (Chico: CA: Scholars Press, 1981), pp. 63-79.

[2.] See S. Talmon, "The Biblical Concept of Jerusalem," *Journal of Ecumenical Studies* 8 (1971), 300-16.

[3.] See J. A. Seeligman, "Jerusalem in Jewish-Hellenistic Thought," *Judah and Jerusalem* (The Twelfth Archaeological Convention; Jerusalem: Israel Exploration Society, 1957), pp. 196-98 [Hebrew].

A Heritage, A History:
The City Of David Exhibition

On June 29, 1987, I received a telephone call from Yigal Shiloh. At the time, he was teaching on sabbatical at Duke University in Durham, N. C. In addition to its program in archaeology, Duke had a special attraction: the superb cancer treatment center at Duke University Hospital.

Yigal and I had often talked about my interviewing him for *Biblical Archaeology Review*, but he had always been too busy directing the dig, processing the finds, administering an organization, and writing technical scientific papers. A year and half earlier, this healthy, strapping hulk of a man had suddenly been struck with stomach cancer. An operation that removed two-thirds of his stomach came too late; the cancer had spread. Now he was calling to ask if I wanted to do an interview.

In less than 24 hours, I was in Durham. Yigal's wife Tami met me at the airport, but she did not prepare me for what I was to see—a frail, wraith of a man. Yet, he had not given up hope; there was a new procedure—a bone marrow transplant—that he thought might save his life.

"Even when you're close to giving up," he told me, "you get to a point where you ask yourself, 'What's next?' And what's next is not giving up. As long as there is a solution—it's really a tough fight—but it's not a lost fight. Statistically, some say there's nothing there. But whatever I can do, I'm doing. I don't see why I shouldn't fight all the way. Next week I'll be 50 years old. My life was never easy. But I have always done things. Now it's really frustrating. I cannot control things. I'd like to do everything I can. And who knows what."

For five hours we talked into a tape recorder. His voice was thin and weak, but his thoughts were as strong and vigorous as ever.[*]

He never regained sufficient strength to undergo the bone marrow procedure. A few months later, he returned to Jerusalem. He wanted to be in Jerusalem, his home. Two weeks after he returned, he was awarded the prestigious Jerusalem Prize in Archaeology. The presentation was made at his bedside by Jerusalem Mayor Teddy Kollek. A week later, Yigal Shiloh died.

Shiloh was a leader of the second generation of Israeli archaeologists. A sabra, a paratrooper, a brilliant student, an inspiring teacher, he was always eager to adopt into his work the latest scientific advances and insightful new archaeological perspectives.

His excavation in the City of David (*Ir David*) was the third major dig in Jerusalem since Israel reunited Jerusalem in the Six-Day War of 1967. The first was led by the doyen of Israeli archaeologists, Benjamin Mazar, south and southwest of the Temple Mount. The second was directed by the highly regarded paleographer and archaeologist Nahman Avigad, who dug in the Jewish Quarter of the Old City as the area was being rebuilt after the 19-year Jordanian occupation. Neither of these digs was easy or uncomplicated. But neither was as demanding as the precipitous, rocky slope of the City of David. When it was decided to dig in a third major area, the City of David, a vigorous younger archaeologist was sought.

The City of David, a 12-acre ridge south of the Temple Mount, is the oldest inhabited part of Jerusalem. Canaanites lived here (and only in this area of Jerusalem) for 2,000 years before King David captured the city in about 1000 B.C.E. Naturally protected by steep slopes on three sides, supplied with water by a perennial spring, and sited on the only passable north-south highway in central Canaan, Jerusalem was destined for greatness—historically and archaeologically. It is easily the most excavated city in the world. For 150 years explorers and diggers have come here to learn about their—our—heritage. All the great names have been here—the American orientalist Edward Robinson; Charles Warren of the London-based Palestine Exploration Fund; Frederick J. Bliss and A. C. Dickie; the Irish archaeologist R. A. S. Macalister; the infamous Parker expedition that searched for Temple treasures; Raymond Weill, a French Jew whom some think excavated the tomb of King David himself; and the distinguished British archaeologist Kathleen Kenyon, who dug in the City of David from 1961 to 1967. This by no means exhausts the list. In a 1975 article, Shiloh himself listed 56 archaeological expeditions in Jerusalem since 1863.

When Kathleen Kenyon finished digging in the City of David in 1967, she declared there was nothing more to find. To anyone else who wanted to dig in that picked-over pile of rocks she wished good luck.

Yigal Shiloh accepted the challenge. The extraordinary results of his eight seasons of excavation are summarized by Gila Hurvitz in the Introduction and by Roberta Maltese in her chronicle of the excavation. It would take volumes to discuss them all.

Nothing was too small or insignificant to engage Yigal Shiloh's attention. And he was quick to bring in experts from all kinds of disciplines to help understand and interpret what he had found. I will mention only one example, which I think he would have enjoyed (he was not a pompous man).

Among his discoveries were a couple of beautifully carved stone toilet seats. [See Photo 10.] So we even know something about the bathroom habits of our ancestors. But there was more. The refuse from one of the cesspits was analyzed. From the fecal deposits, experts have been able to deduce the diet and diseases of the residents of the city. From this, historians have been able to speculate about the food supply as the Babylonians tightened their vise on the city shortly before they burned and destroyed Jerusalem in 586 B.C.E.

Sadly, Yigal did not live to write a final report. Yet, even if he had, it would have been a joint effort of many scholars in many disciplines, as well as of the archaeologists who worked with him. They will simply have to carry on without their leader. Already the first volumes are beginning to appear. What we will miss most, however, is the expansive creativity he would have brought to the entire project—to see it whole on the broad canvas of history. For, as he was concerned with the smallest detail, so he always had before him the big picture. Somehow we will have to rely on his inspiration to complete the vision.

Hershel Shanks

[*]This interview appeared in the March/April and May/June 1988 issues of *Biblical Archaeology Review*.

EXCAVATING THE FIRST BIBLICAL ROYAL CITY 1978-1985: A CHRONICLE

Nearly 3,000 years ago, David, the psalmist and passionate warrior-king of the Hebrew Bible, friend to Jonathan and slayer of the Philistine Goliath, conquered the City of Jebus and transformed it into the capital of his United Kingdom. David built a house of cedarwood from Lebanon on the city's perilously steep slope. It was from that house that he spied Bathsheba, who would bear his son and successor, Solomon. In that house he grieved for another son, his beloved Absalom.

Tradition had held that David's city was on Jerusalem's western hill, "Mount Zion," but many archaeologists rejected the possibility because it lacked a perennial water supply, critical to permanent settlement. The eastern hill has the Gihon Spring.

In July 1978, a team from the Institute of Archaeology at the Hebrew University mounted an eight-year excavation on Jerusalem's southeastern slope to investigate the material remains of the City of David. The site is first mentioned in II Samuel: "And David dwelt in the stronghold and called it the city of David" [5:9]. It is the oldest part of Jerusalem and central to stories the Jews have preserved for thousands of years. Those stories, in the telling and retelling, have taken on a hallowed luster, such as human handling leaves on a stone tool over time.

Creating the Expedition

The late Dr. Yigal Shiloh, director of the Institute's excavation, was responsible for organizing, recording, and supervising the work on the site's 15 dunams (a dunam is about 3/4 of an acre). Administering a project the size of the City of David and doing the science involved demanded experience, scrupulous recordkeeping, energy, authority, and a thick skin. Shiloh had them all.

The details of the job were daunting: selecting and supervising a staff of about 30; overseeing a rotating cadre of more than 300 mostly inexperienced volunteers each season; assessing where to cut trenches; recording, registering, and researching artifacts and architectural elements (in collaboration with staff and colleagues in diverse disciplines); maintaining a public relations effort with the local and foreign press, the excavation's Arab

neighbors, the excavation's sponsors, and religious and government authorities; and publishing the findings and conclusions.

In 1978, following aerial and ground surveys, Shiloh opened operations by dividing the excavatable land into five areas, each designated by a letter of the alphabet. The land is all state-owned, some having been purchased by Baron Edmond de Rothschild before the First World War. Ownership was transferred to the State of Israel in 1954. A much smaller amount of land, now also public, had originally been purchased by the British Mandatory authority.

Shiloh was aware from the outset that in the 10th century B.C.E. the dimensions of the southeastern hill had not exceeded 30 dunams. This suggested that, to build a royal city, the planners would have had to utilize all of the slope. Therefore, to the extent that it could be done—given the modern and topological boundaries—Shiloh and his team would be excavating the entire slope and its tiers of terraces.

The City of David

The City of David overlooks the Kidron Valley, outside the 16th-century walls of the Old City, southeast of the sacred Temple Mount. [14] The Temple Mount is biblical Mount Moriah, where Abraham consented to sacrifice his son, Isaac. It is where Solomon, in 968 B.C.E., built a splendid temple to the Lord on land David had purchased from a Jebusite called Araunah. Herod built the Second Temple there, the temple Jesus knew. To Moslems the Temple Mount is the Haram es-Sharif, "the noble sanctuary," and the spot from which Muhammad ascended to heaven on his horse, al-Buraq. Since the 7th century C.E., it has housed the Dome of the Rock and the el-Aqsa Mosque, which was, in the 12th century, the Crusaders' *Templum Domini*.

14. Aerial view of the Kidron Valley below the Temple Mount (top center). The City of David is in the center of the photo, on the S.E. slope, across from the modern village of Silwan (bottom right).

Access to the City of David excavation was from a steep side street, Wadi Hilwe. The street is pitched at a 45-degree angle off of the Ophel Road, which runs alongside the Temple Mount and in front of the Dung Gate. The neighborhood is residential and Moslem and, in municipal terms, part of the village of Silwan across the valley. The excavation rented two houses adjacent to the site from a Silwan resident, a negotiation renewed each year. The protocol for the transaction required at least a full day of coffee and tea drinking for the parties involved.

In the expedition's first season, newly opened squares revealed a tawny monochrome at the top of the slope of a Hasmonean (Hellenistic) fortification element and biblical foundation stones. The surrounding

ERRATA

Editor's Note: Producing an illustrated book in two months, when its contributors are at a daunting geographic distance from each other and from the book's designer and printer, invites errata. The following omissions and corrections did not reach the printer until after the book had gone to press.

• The map drawn by the book's designer for the cover and the text panels is from *The Living Bible* (Wheaton, Ill.: Tyndale House Publishers, 1976).

• Talma Levin designed the original exhibition installation in Jerusalem.

• The plans and drawings reproduced in the text are by Shifra Eisenstein, Sara Halbreich, Leen Ritmeyer, Wolf Schleicher, and Ada Yardeni.

• Page 13, line 23: A dunam is equivalent to 1/4 of an acre.

• Pages 14 and 20: The designations S.E. and Southeast should read "southeastern."

• Photo 15, page 15: The caption assumes four-color printing.

• Page 15, line 7: Jerusalem was destroyed during the reign of King Zedekiah.

• Photo 17, page 16: This photograph is on its side. Correctly placed the measure is to the left.

modern houses in Silwan are that color, as are all the buildings in Jerusalem. A municipal law, in effect since the British Mandate, requires them to be faced with Jerusalem limestone. In summer, it is the color—or absence of it—of the Judean Desert to the southeast. [See Photo 23.]

David's modest city had been enlarged and embellished by Solomon and subsequent kings of Judah. But it was the city destroyed during the reign of King Yehoiakim, in 586 B.C.E., on the ninth of the Hebrew month of *Ab*, by the army of the Babylonian king Nebuchadnezzar, that occupied the excavating team in Area G for several seasons. The exile of King Yehoiakim to Babylon (modern Iraq) is reported in II Chronicles 36:5-6; the exile of the people is recalled in Psalm 137: "By the rivers of Babylon, There we sat down, yea, we wept, When we remembered Zion."

The southeastern hill had already been excavated piecemeal several times before the arrival of the Institute's team, most recently, from 1961-1967, by the prominent British archaeologist Dame Kathleen Kenyon. The eastern part of Jerusalem was then under the hegemony of the Hashemite Kingdom of Jordan. Kenyon's partial excavation had led her to some premature conclusions the Israelis' findings would revise.

The city's history of destruction by its enemies, earthquakes, and erosion from heavy winter rains over millennia, in addition to the number of times it had been investigated, left the Israeli team with few illusions about the possibility of royal buildings or priestly dwellings emerging from the hill. But there was hope that the stones themselves would echo what once had been.

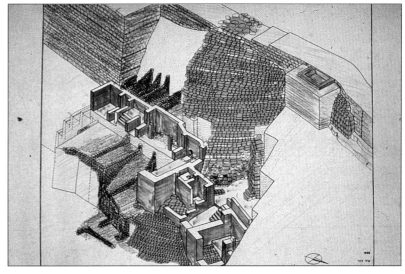

15. Isometric reconstruction of the stratigraphical phases in Area G: Gray-brown walls and surrounding fills = the substructure of the stepped-stone structure. Yellow courses of stone = superstructure of the stone structure, interpreted as the lower reaches of a Jebusite fortress or citadel. Red-orange walls = residential buildings built in the 8th–7th centuries B.C.E. on top of the stone structure and destroyed in 586 B.C.E. Blue fortification wall and tower at the eastern edge of the hill = fortification wall constructed during the Second Temple period, when the city's eastern boundary was moved from midslope to the crest.

The Stepped-Stone Structure

The end of the second season witnessed a very loud echo of what had been. Digging deeper on the slope than any team before it, the Israelis found that the cyclopean stones of the stepped-stone structure Kenyon had found hugging the crest in Area G were originating from under the Israelite residences built against it. [See Photo 5.] The team was able to date the pottery they found on top of the structure to the Early Iron Age, the 10th century B.C.E., the city of the Jebusites and David. They had reached the level of the royal city.

Two years later, they uncovered a system of stone-filled compartments underlying the "steps." Sherds retrieved from the compartments, from a clearly defined archaeological context, were dated to the 13th-12th century B.C.E. The massive stepped-stone structure at the top of the slope could now be understood to have supported the acropolis in the city David conquered, an acropolis his builders reused. [15]

16. Israelite "proto-aeolic" or palmette capital found by Kenyon in the City of David.

The discovery was all the more encouraging because beneath the crest, in the Israelite level, not far from the structure, Kenyon had found a fragment of a pilaster capital. Its style was identical to capital fragments from other royal cities of the period. Optimism grew. It looked as though some of the gaps in the grudging record would be filled. [16]

Building Stones, Terracing, and Inscriptions

At the crest of the hill, the single narrow trench Kenyon dug had exposed the well-preserved infrastructure of a four-room house, ubiquitous in the country in the Israelite period (1200-600 B.C.E.). There, too, the Israelis expanded on Kenyon's research. In the debris of the house, they uncovered a partially intact storage jar on which the name "Ahiel" had been written in ink. [See Photo 9.] The House of Ahiel, as it came to be known, also produced an inscribed ashlar, a worked building stone. [See Photo 11.]

17. Close-up of the header-stretcher, roughly hewn ashlars used in a large building (12 x 13 m) in Area E, known as the Ashlar House. The building's construction and topographical placement — over two upper terraces — suggest that it served a public function.

Throughout the slope, Kenyon's trench exposed terracing, the method of construction devised by town planners in the Iron Age to support houses and public buildings on a steep hill. At the bottom of her trench—midway down the slope but above the water source (the Gihon Spring)—Kenyon had exposed about 40 meters of the city's earliest boundary, a fortification wall built on the bedrock. She dated it to the Middle Bronze II period (ca. 1800 B.C.E.). In 1979, their second season in the field, the Israelis uncovered another 35 meters and confirmed Kenyon's dating. The Bronze Age city wall is still visible, buttressing the terraces, at varying heights, or courses of stones. [See Photos 3 and 4.] It was the Israelis' Area E of excavation. [17]

In 1978, a volunteer had found a fragment of an inscribed stone plaque in a dump in Area E thought to have been deposited not long after the destruction of Jerusalem by the Romans in 70 C.E. [18] An inscription is a special find. Through analysis of the letter shapes, an epigrapher can estimate, with only a small margin for error, when the inscription was written. The Hebrew letters of the Area E inscription resembled those on a funerary inscription found in the village of Silwan across the valley and on the plaque found on the wall in Hezekiah's Tunnel, one of the three water systems in the slope connected with the spring. Both of those inscriptions had been dated to the end of the 8th century B.C.E. The paleographic similarity of the Area E inscription suggested that the plaque also should be dated to the reign of Hezekiah or to the later kings of Judah.

The hewn tunnel would have enabled Hezekiah's city to withstand the anticipated siege by the Assyrian king Sennacherib in 701. The plaque commemorates the hewers' task and technique. Another version of the story of how Hezekiah's challenge from the boastful Assyrian tyrant was met is told in the book of Isaiah [37: 33-37].

18. Inscribed plaque, found in an Area E dump. The fragmentary inscription suggests that someone "heaped up" or "accumulated" something, language used in the Bible with commodities or precious metals.

The Science of Destruction

Archaeology is the science of destruction, which made controlled excavation by stratum and the systematic recording of everything excavated essential practices in the field. The order of excavation—from the most recent occupation level to the earliest—makes it impossible to return to what was. The technique of stratigraphic excavation was pioneered in Palestine by Sir Flinders-Petrie, an Egyptologist, in 1890, at another biblical site, Tel el-Hesi.

In the City of David, as elsewhere, when a level of occupation was excavated, everything in it was reproduced in the dig architect's plans and the surveyor's section drawings: walls, floors, objects, levels, architectural elements. Although the excavation also had a staff photographer, a photograph limits details and perspective; a drawing renders simultaneously the level that has vanished and the new level reached.

19. Pottery group from the House of Ahiel.

To reconstruct a stratum, the team had to perform meticulous recordkeeping because frequently stratification was complicated—where stones were reused, terraces intruded, floors were worn away, and pits had been dug. In addition, the archaeologists recorded all the debris and objects of daily use human habitation had created on the slope, paying special attention to the sequences of pottery types.

The City of David excavation, like others, was a laboratory for its staff. They tested their hypotheses and applied their methodology, stratigraphical analysis and pottery chronology. The body of knowledge made available by the excavation and by others like it is expanding exponentially.

The Ceramic Evidence

In the City of David, the period best represented in terms of quantity of pottery is that of the Israelite kings. [19] Significant advances have been made in the last 20 years in constructing a pottery typology for the United Kingdom of Judah. Today, the City of David staff is making important contributions to such a typology in the series of reports now being published, in English, by the Institute of Archaeology.

Batches of stamped *la melekh* handles, from storage jars "belonging to the king," form part of the City of David ceramic collection. These handles have been found elsewhere in the country—at Lachish, for example—in the stratum destroyed by Sennacherib in 701. It is presumed that the jars had something to do with the collection of taxes, but more than that is as yet unclear. A provocative feature of the *la melekh* handles is that they share a clay type, or chemical profile. That information was determined by having samples of the handles irradiated in a nuclear reactor, a tool that was not available to early practitioners of archaeology.

In general, the development of a chronological sequence for Syro-Palestinian pottery is also credited to Flinders-Petrie. Even today, despite new and experimental technologies, students of Syro-Palestinian archaeology must master ceramic sequences.

Archaeology and Politics in the Holy City

The City of David was not a typical tell—one of the isolated artificial mounds that dot Israel's valleys and wilderness. It is part of a living city and as such presented special topographical problems to its excavators. Specifically, those problems were limited open space on a steep slope and the modern houses inhabited by the residents of Silwan.

A few weeks into the 1981 season, however, the ancient core of Jerusalem presented problems to the Hebrew University team that were unrelated to quirky topography or previous excavations. The City of David became front-page news all over the world. Jerusalem, home to the plain and the pious, prophets and priests, is also home to zealots. No sooner had the unique stepped-stone structure been dated than Shiloh received demands that the digging in Area G stop.

On August 3, 1981, about 70 male and female pietists from the *Naturei Karta*, Aramaic for "Keepers of the City," stormed Area G, overturned buckets of pottery sherds, flung tools, wrestled the area supervisor to the ground, and attacked the director, an ex-paratrooper. The *Naturei Karta* asserted that Area G had been a cemetery in the Middle Ages and that the archaeologists were desecrating Jewish graves. The real issue, understood by all, was paramountcy in the State of Israel: Would it be religious or secular? Which should prevail had already been an issue: when the prophet Samuel reluctantly anointed Israel's first king, Saul, whom David succeeded. Despite the daily drama at its gates—the stones and imprecations of menacing hordes of protesters and the bustling of the international media and Jerusalem's mounted police—work in all areas but G continued. The archaeologists had their day in the Knesset, led by the late Professor Yigael Yadin, which upheld their right to excavate. The prime minister at the time, Menachem Begin, was reported to have commented wryly, "Israel does not have enough problems, so it goes digging for them." Shiloh and his staff grew sanguine about the intrusion, perhaps because there is inherent in events in Jerusalem a persistent strain of *déja vu*.

Silwan: The Neighborhood

"The Hajj," a burly, middle-aged man, was the local resident of Silwan whose two houses Shiloh negotiated use of each year. He was called Hajj (a Moslem who has made the pilgrimage to Mecca) by some of the staff but never by Shiloh. It was an audacious bid for acknowledgment on the part of the staff that only succeeded after years of encounters.

To visiting Westerners, the Hajj was the neighbor who barked at the local children in Arabic and at the staff in Hebrew, in a voice that was an unmodulated assault on the ears. The children, of course, had been drawn to his yard by the sight of the volunteers washing broken pottery under a large red tarpaulin. Although the Hajj patrolled the courtyard the team's rented houses shared with the house he and his extended family lived in, he was not curious about the activities there. He patrolled because he was vigilant about his property, and he had good reason; too-exuberant college kids stepped in his garden and sat on his stone walls. They were a nuisance, like the children.

But the residents of Silwan were not defined by the Hajj. A housewife who lived just above the northern limit of Area G, below the walls of the Old City and the Temple Mount, every hot August bridged mutually alien languages and cultures. She would send one of her young sons down the slope—he would inch his way down with the toe-hold of a mountain goat—with her silver tea service on a silver tray. It held either a pot of sweetened mint tea or steamy, thick coffee with cardamon and a set of tiny glasses.

The boy would set the gleaming tray on newly excavated stones and, in the assembled company of his brothers, sisters, and friends, watch as the volunteers drank. His mother waved from her backyard. The grateful volunteers, introduced to traditional Arab hospitality, waved back, their wide waves mimicking the exaggerated gestures of actors on a stage.

The Hajj did visit Area G once, and it was a display of interest. He was showing around a *mukhtar*, or "head man," of a nearby village who was curious about the daily TV coverage the excavation was getting. It was 1981, the year the archaeology community collided with the *Naturei Karta*. The *mukhtar* knew that, for the Jews, a nerve was being struck.

Excavating David's City

Early morning on Wadi Hilwe in East Jerusalem is still and cool. The air is not yet heavy with the warring odors from the overflowing garbage in the green metal bins the municipal trucks may or may not empty that day. Only the villagers' first stirrings—the clatter of pots or the braying of a donkey— break the stillness. Soon the recorded voice of a muezzin will call the faithful to prayer from a stone minaret up near the Intercontinental Hotel on the Mount of Olives.

20. *Silwan and the view out toward the wilderness of Judea from the City of David. The modern houses in Silwan are built following the configuration of the bedrock, as were the houses on the Southeast hill in the Iron Age.*

The City of David and the village of Silwan that mirrors it across the Kidron Valley are in shade. In a couple of hours both will be locked in the white grip of the Levantine sun. From the edge of the eastern slope, one can see northeast to the Mount of Olives, across to Absalom's Tomb and Silwan, and south toward the beginning of the Wilderness of Judea. The sun is ahead, its first rays just long and strong enough to bathe the leaves on the Hajj's lemon tree. [20]

The excavation team began to assemble at about 6:15; it began to work at 6:30. For some excavations that would be a late start, but this dig was in a city. Without a camp to house them, volunteers and staff were scattered in a variety of living arrangements. People arrived in private cars (consumptive Fiats led in popularity) or on foot.

By 6:15, then, the volunteers were clustering in loose groups, filling their canteens with water or stashing their belongings in the Volunteer House rented from the Hajj. There wasn't much talk beyond "Good morning," *Boker tov*, in Hebrew. The volunteers waited for their supervisors, graduate students at the Institute. The supervisors were in the Staff House, also rented from the Hajj, getting the day's marching orders from Shiloh. Shiloh would later visit each of the areas, some time before the 9:30 break, for an update on progress and problems. He was available for both by walkie-talkie.

Into the Field

The clatter of transits, hand tools, drawing boards, and empty pottery buckets announced the arrival of the supervisors in the courtyard and the move to the field. The hardiest of the volunteers pushed wheelbarrows loaded with *patiches*, "small hand picks," pickaxes, shovels, brushes, and *guffas*—Arabic for "basket." The *guffas*, fashioned from used tires, were used to haul soil and rocks out of the field in bone-wearying rounds of fill-and-dump.

Not all staff and volunteers worked in the sun. Some toiled by the light of a bare bulb to empty the debris-filled Warren's Shaft, a water system, like Hezekiah's Tunnel, connected to the Gihon Spring. Some believe the shaft was the *tsinnor*, or "gutter," David used to overtake the Jebusite city [II Samuel 5:8]. In the dig's third season, the volunteer corps in the shaft included two South African mining engineers and a few local mountain climbers. The result of their labor is that Warren's Shaft is now open to the public and incorporated into a small site museum. [**21**]

21. Warren's Shaft: Midway down the Southeast hill, one enters a rock-cut, sloping tunnel to the strategic underground water system connected to the Gihon Spring. A horizontal tunnel ahead leads to a verticle shaft that descends to a channel, also rock-cut, carrying water from the Spring. The entrance to this system was inside the Iron Age city wall.

Out of the Field

Any volunteer feeling averse to being in the sun on any given day could sit under the red tarpaulin and wash sherds from the previous day's fieldwork. Hundreds of sherds came out of the ground daily; they were placed in buckets tagged with the area designation, the date, and the level at which they were found. The sherds to be washed would have been sitting in a bucket of water overnight, to loosen any soil adhering to them. Usually only representative pieces—diagnostic sherds—were kept: rims, handles, glazed, burnished, or incised sherds, and sherds of apparently similar contour, color, and fabric (finish, clay, or weight) that might be part of the same piece and restorable. Many thousands of sherds were discarded each season.

Volunteers scrubbed the sherds with fine brushes, placed them in wood or plastic trays, and set the trays on the low walls in the Hajj's courtyard to dry in the sun. There was a pottery "reading" every day after lunch. The supervisors would set the trays, full of the sherds and small finds from their areas—glass, jewelry, coins, loom weights, spindle whorls, metal fragments, and carved stone, bone, and ivory—in front of Shiloh, in much the same way that tribute was probably once set before Caesar.

22. Pottery "reading." Dig director Yigal Shiloh (far right) with staff.

Shiloh's fingers would fly over the pieces, flipping them or raising one for an instant, as he called out their period of origin—Middle Bronze II, 8th century, Persian, Hellenistic, Roman, Byzantine, Islamic, Turkish—always looking for the intrusive piece, a piece out of historical, or chronological, order. Intrusive material negates the scientific integrity of its locus, or find spot, and makes the material unusable in a research report. [22]

The pieces the team kept were subsequently registered: marked with India ink, in a code that included their area, by letter; basket number; the year; and the Hebrew acronym *ayn dalet*, which stands for *Ir David*, the "City of David." A registration code simplifies both pottery restoration and the retrieval of artifacts for research and exhibition.

The volunteers' day ended by 12:30, but not the staff's. At least three times a week staff members lectured to the group on special interests: ceramic typologies, restoration, numismatics, the water systems, the history of the site. Only after the last exhausted volunteer had struggled up Wadi Hilwe in the direction of the Old City did the staff have lunch. Lunch was al fresco, at makeshift tables under the Hajj's grape arbor. In the afternoon, without the physical volume of the volunteers, the slope seemed desolate. The heat continued to suffuse the air, while a light, independent breeze wafted the heavy perfume of the jasmine growing in the courtyard.

The New Archaeology

The City of David expedition left the field in 1985. The team had identified and/or reevaluated four of the city's walls in different historical periods, as well as many unique artifacts and architectural features. The significance of that material, relative to other material excavated at other sites, will continue to be studied for years to come, because archaeology is a comparative discipline and new information is always being made available. Some of the evidence will always be elusive or lost—lacunae in the archaeological record that frustrate researchers.

The new archaeology, which is interdisciplinary, was practiced at the City of David: an unusual object first dated in an archaeological context was sent to a specialist for analysis. Experts in a variety of disciplines—zoology, geology, anthropology, Bible and extrabiblical studies, paleography, chemistry—assisted Shiloh and his team. In collaboration, inscriptions were deciphered, unique and rare objects identified, and texts linked to the material in the archaeological record.

Past, Present, Future

Jerusalem's antiquities and holy places and the stories they recall are at the heart of our collective religious and cultural memory. The stories, rich with moral authority, live in language as metaphor and as inspiration for art.

As a physical reality, Jerusalem has been accessible to all since the founding of the State of Israel in 1948. Today, an archaeological park, which begins at the Jaffa Gate, inside the medieval walls of the Old City, incorporates David's city. The residential quarter in Area G that Nebuchadnezzar destroyed in the 6th century B.C.E. has been restored. It sits against the Canaanite stepped-stone structure David's engineers reused to build his city's acropolis. [See Photo 5.]

The City of David's eight seasons of dust and heat are embedded in the memory of everyone who worked on it, for the intense physicality of digging does that. The staff, drawn from graduate students at the Hebrew University's Institute of Archaeology, reflected Israel's diverse demographic makeup: they were Sabras, American and South African *olim*, "new immigrants," and an Israeli Arab. Volunteers came from the United States, Canada, Europe, South Africa, South America, Japan, Australia, and Israel. People were there because of the stories—and for the archaeology, of course. Some came just for a tan. Many returned season after season, not a few of whom used the word *privileged* to describe how they felt about working there, and used it unabashedly.

The excavation, in which sacred and world history were explored, itself officially became a part of the history of Jerusalem with this exhibition. Its dramatic recoveries, its almost daily confrontations with the complex passions identified with tradition, and surely the untimely death of the man whose name became synonymous with his excavation, now pass into the realm of story, of history. Let it be understood that all that happened there, in one guise or another, happened for the love of Jerusalem, the most human of all cities, the psalmist's city, the city with the wilderness at its gate. [23]

Roberta B. Maltese

23. Area G, 1979, the Hasmonean glacis, looking north toward the wall of the Old City of Jerusalem and the Mount of Olives.

THE HOUSE OF THE BULLAE

*T*hen did Baruch read in the book the words of Jeremiah in the house of the Lord, in the chamber of Gemariah the son of Shaphan the scribe [to King Jehoiakim of Judah] in the upper court, at the entry of the new gate of the Lord's house, in the ears of all the people. [Jeremiah 36:10]

The City of David, Summer 1982

It is early morning in the City of David. The heat is already beginning to creep up from the desert at the city's feet. The light breeze that may intermittently break into the morning will be a mere wisp. More than 100 volunteers and at least a dozen staff members from the Institute of Archaeology are at work on the slope. They will be grateful for any relief from the heat. They are excavating the city that David, the second king of Israel, conquered from the Jebusites, in about 1000 B.C.E.

The clink of metal tools against stone, the crunch of the wheelbarrows meeting rocky soil, and the hum of voices in more than one language echo across the Kidron Valley to the modern Arab village of Silwan, which is still half in shadow. From a loudspeaker in the minaret near the ancient Jewish cemetery on the Mount of Olives, a muezzin's thin, nasal wail is calling Moslems to prayer. The sounds of the awakening village will begin to echo back across the valley.

We are in Area G, at the top of the steep southeastern slope, standing in the shadow cast by a five-foot-high wooden wall Israel's ultra-orthodox community has forced the archaeologists to construct. It is Israel's newest border, and the archaeologists may not dig beyond it in Area G.

An experienced volunteer is working alone to clean the plaster floor of a room in a structure destroyed in 586 B.C.E. by Nebuchadenezzar's army. Only the building's infrastructure remains—its walls and ash-covered plaster floor. The thick deposit of ash is an indicator of destruction by fire. The arrowheads and charred organic remains stuck in the ash are indicators of violent destruction. The debris had been sealed for more than two millennia by a glacis, a fortification element, constructed by the Hasmonean kings in the second century B.C.E.

The volunteer works slowly, cautiously approaching the plaster and ash, a lot of ash, on the lookout for small finds—an earring, an arrowhead, a bead, perhaps. With one hand he directs the tip of his *patiche* (Hebrew for a "hand

25

pick," but actually a trowel-like tool), lightly, with restraint; with the other he flicks the fine bristles of a brush over the surface of the floor. Some of the ash and plaster appears to have bonded in small clumps. He picks up a handful and studies them in his palm. Each is tenaciously harboring something in its core—maybe only a pebble. He taps one. The ash falls away to reveal a nearly oval disc of baked clay, less than half an inch in diameter. With his thumb he rubs the surface ash. He works up some spittle to help ease off the rest. Something is inscribed in the clay.

The volunteer calls to David Tarler and Jane Cahill, the Area G supervisors. Palming the lump of clay, Tarler, too, gently rubs it surface. It is a bulla, an impression made by a carved seal on a lump of wet clay.

The supervisors excitedly sent for Yigal Shiloh, as volunteers and staff began to surround them. Shiloh came running, his cameras flapping around his neck. Expectation was visceral, rippling through the morning's heavy heat.

A second bulla emerged, and then a third. More bullae. More inscriptions. Shiloh dispersed the crowd that had gathered and joined the volunteer at the findspot in the room in front of the five-foot-high wall. "Bring a sifter," he shouted to Tarler, "we don't want to miss anything here."

Altogether they would uncover 51 bullae—41 of them legible, four uninscribed but bearing designs. [24] A paleographer from the Hebrew University was called in. He read the names in their biblical Hebrew as if he were reading them in *Ha Aretz*, one of Israel's daily newspapers:

"Benayahu son of Hosha'yahu, Gemaryahu son of Shaphan ... ."

"Gemaryahu." It was the name of the son of Shaphan, the scribe in the court of King Yehoiakim, in whose chamber, "in the upper court, at the entry of the new gate of the Lord's house, in the ears of all the people," Baruch had read the words of Jeremiah. The time was not long before the arrival of Nebuchadenezzar's army, which would destroy the city and exile its population "beside the

24. Assemblage of City of David bullae. The average size is 14 x 12 x 2.6 mm. Most have impressions of personal, formulaic seals: "Belonging to X, Son of Y" from the 7th–6th centuries B.C.E. Impressions of both the string that tied the rolled papyrus and the textured papyrus itself appear on the seal's reverse.

waters of Babylon." From that time onward, the earthly Jerusalem, Zion, would become, in word and memory, the focus of the historico-political dream of the exiled Jews.

Shiloh speculated that the room in which the bullae had been preserved, so close to the Temple Mount, just to the north, might have been part of Jerusalem's administrative center. Important documents, written on papyrus, would have been stored there. [25] They would have been sealed by important royal functionaries. Pressed into the reverse of each of the bullae was an impression from the papyrus scroll the clay had once sealed. The fires set by Nebuchadnezzar's army had burned the papyrus, but they had baked the clay, preserving it.

Roberta B. Maltese

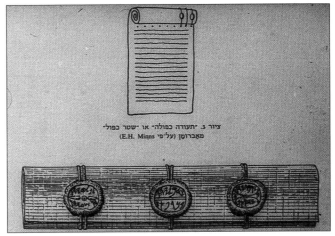

25. Reconstruction: A document sealed with bullae.

EXHIBITION CHECKLIST

Explanation and sample entry:

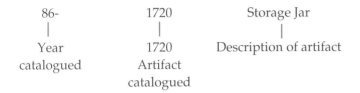

I. MIDDLE BRONZE AGE II   18th - 16th centuries B.C.E.

86-1720 Storage Jar
86-1733 Juglet
86-1922 Bone Inlay (4)
86-1923 Antler
86-1924 Bone Inlay
86-1926 Bone Object
86-1927 Bone Inlay
86-1928 Bone Inlay
86-1929 Bone Inlay
86-1930 Bone Object
86-1931 Gaming Piece
86-1932 Bone Inlay
86-2017 Juglet
89-1151 Scarab
89-1154 Scarab
89-1168 Stamped Handle
89-1170 Stamped Handle

II. IRON AGE   12th - 7th centuries B.C.E.

80-840   Inscribed Stone (Replica)
86-0406 Figurine
86-0408 Figurine
86-0409 Figurine
86-0411 Figurine
86-0412 Figurine
86-0413 Figurine
86-0414 Figurine
86-0415 Figurine
86-0416 Figurine

Bone objects, Middle Bronze Age: (L.)
Carved inlays with motifs common to the
period. (R. and bottom) Buttons (?),
gaming pieces, unworked horn.

86-0417 Figurine
86-0418 Figurine
86-0419 Figurine
86-0420 Figurine
86-1785 Chalice
86-1786 Chalice
86-1839 Figurine
86-1844 Figurine
86-1846 Figurine
86-1851 Figurine
86-1854 Figurine
86-1855 Figurine
86-1859 Figurine
86-1872 Figurine
86-1874 Figurine
86-1881 Figurine
86-1887 Figurine
86-1889 Figurine
86-1901 Figurine
86-1904 Figurine
86-2018 Cult Stand
86-2019 Bronze Fist
86-2026 Figurine
86-2027 Figurine
86-2028 Figurine
86-2029 Figurine
86-2030 Figurine
86-2031 Figurine
86-2032 Figurine
86-2033 Figurine

THE BURNT HOUSE/AREA G
86-0341 Juglet
86-0350 Plate
86-0351 Plate
86-0356 Small Plate
86-0359 Plate
86-0363 Lamp
86-0365 Bowl
86-0366 Bowl
86-0370 Juglet
86-0381 Cooking Pot

Pottery figurine.

86-0387 Storage Jar
86-0389 Krater
86-0395 Loom Weight
86-0396 Pilgrim Flask
86-0403 Bone Object
86-0432 Pendant
86-0433 Pendant
86-0640 Arrowhead
86-0643 Arrowhead
86-0644 Arrowhead
86-0645 Arrowhead
86-0649 Arrowhead
86-0652 Carbonized Wood
86-0653 Carbonized Wood
86-0654 Jug
86-1702 Storage Jar
86-1735 Bowl
86-1736 Bowl
86-1737 Bowl
86-1758 Cooking Pot
86-1759 Krater
86-1784 Stand
86-1790 Stone Weight
86-1791 Stone Weight
86-1792 Grinding Stone
86-1793 Stone Weight
86-1796 Button
86-1798 Button
86-2023/1 Loom Weight
86-2023/2 Loom Weight
86-2023/3 Loom Weight
86-2023/4 Loom Weight
86-2023/5 Loom Weight

THE HOUSE OF AHIEL/AREA G
86-0344 Cooking Pot
86-0353 Bowl
86-0357 Bowl
86-0371 Juglet
86-0383 Pilgrim Flask
86-0393 Storage Jar
86-0394 Inscribed Stone (Replica)

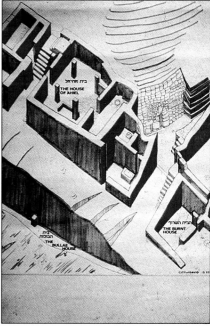

Isometric reconstruction of Area G: the House of Ahiel, the Burnt House (north), and the House of the Bullae (east).

86-0400   Bead
86-0421   Hebrew Ostraca
86-0453   Bead
86-1704   Krater
86-1705   Storage Jar
86-1706   Storage Jar
86-1707   Storage Jar
86-1708   Storage Jar
86-1709   Jar
86-1710   Storage Jar
86-1711   Storage Jar
86-1713   Storage Jar
86-1714   Storage Jar
86-1715   Storage Jar
86-1716   Storage Jar
86-1717   Storage Jar
86-1718   Storage Jar
86-1719   Storage Jar
86-1742   Juglet
86-1743   Lamp
86-1744   Jug
86-1745   Bowl
86-1746   Bowl
86-1747   Bowl
86-1788   Stone Weight
86-1794   Bone Spatula
86-1795   Bone Spatula
86-2050   Storage Jar
86-2051   Stand
86-2052   Bead
86-2053   Bead
Model of the House of Ahiel

THE ASHLAR HOUSE/AREA E

86-0369   Juglet
86-0372   Juglet
86-0380   Stone Jar "Assyrian"
86-0384   Storage Jar
86-0390   Storage Jar
86-1701   Storage Jar
86-1764   Juglet
86-1765   Bowl

86-1767   Bowl
86-2020   Iron Blades
86-2021   Lamp

THE LOWER TERRACE HOUSE/AREA E1

86-0378   Jug
86-1731   Cooking Pot
86-1739   Jug
86-1749   Cooking Krater
86-1754   Cooking Pot
86-1766   Cooking Pot
86-1768   Cooking Pot
86-1769   Cooking Pot
86-1782   Cooking Pot
86-2022   Storage Jar "LMCHMM"

THE HOUSE OF THE BULLAE/AREA G

84-082   Vase
84-083   Vase
84-084   Hole Mouth Jar
84-085   Hole Mouth Jar
84-086   Storage Jar
84-088   Cooking Pot
84-089   Storage Jar
84-090   Stand
84-091   Stand
84-096   Jug
84-097   Jug
84-098   Jug
84-099   Jug
84-100   Juglet
84-101   Altar
84-102   Altar
84-103   Altar
84-104   Altar
84-124   Bulla (Replica)
84-136   Bulla (Replica)
84-137   Bulla (Replica)
84-139   Bulla (Replica)
84-140   Bulla (Replica)
84-143   Bulla (Replica)
84-151   Bulla (Replica)

Bullae: Average size is 14 x 12 x 2.6 mm.

84-154 Bulla (Replica)
84-158 Bulla (Replica)
84-160 Bulla (Replica)
84-162 Bulla (Replica)
84-163 Bulla (Replica)
84-165 Bulla (Replica)
86-1789 Stone Weight
86-2024 Grinding Stone/Weight
86-2025 Grinding Stone

III. PERSIAN PERIOD   6th - 4th centuries B.C.E.

86-1810 Stamped Handle
86-1820 Stamped Handle
86-1828 Stamped Handle
86-1831 Stamped Handle
86-1832 Stamped Body Sherd
86-1833 Stamped Body Sherd
86-2034 Stamped Handle
86-2035 Stamped Handle
86-2036 Stamped Handle
86-2037 Ostraca
86-2038 Ostraca
86-2039 Ostraca
86-2040 Lamp
86-2041 Lamp
86-2042 Gezer Bottle
86-2043 Gezer Bottle
86-2044 Ostraca
86-2045 Stamped Handle
86-2046 Stamped Handle

IV. HELLENISTIC (HASMONEAN) PERIOD Second Half of 2nd century B.C.E.

86-1674 Rhodian Handle
86-1678 Rhodian Handle
86-1680 Rhodian Handle
86-1693 Rhodian Handle
86-1697 Rhodian Handle
86-1698 Rhodian Handle
86-1699 Rhodian Handle
86-1700 Rhodian Handle
86-1805 Stamped Handle
86-2047 Stamped Handle

86-2048 Ostraca
22017 Coin-Ptolemy V
22028 Coin-Antiochus IV
22033 Coin-Antiochus VII
22040 Coin-Alexander Jannaeus
22147 Coin-Mattathias Antigonus

V. EARLY ROMAN (HERODIAN) PERIOD 37 B.C.E. - 70 C.E.

86-0586 Lamp
86-0594 Bottle
86-0595 Bottle
86-0597 Bottle
86-0598 Bottle
86-0599 Bottle
86-1644 Incense Shovel
86-1650 Stone Bowl
86-1651 Measuring Cup
86-1654 Stone Cylinder
86-1655 Lid
86-1667 Juglet
86-1669 Juglet
86-1670 Bottle
86-1671 Bottle
86-1681 Lid
86-1682 Cup Handle
86-1683 Stone Stopper
86-1686 Lamp
86-2049 Ostraca
86-2054 Flute
22157 Coin-Herod I
22162 Coin-Herod Archelaus
22164 Coin-Ambibulus
22171 Coin-Pontius Pilatus
22202 Coin-Festus
22217 Coin-First Jewish War
22219 Coin-First Jewish War

CITY OF DAVID PUBLICATIONS

Shiloh, Y. 1984. *City of David: Interim Report of the First Five Seasons*, vol. 19. Jerusalem: Qedem.

Ariel, D. T. 1990. *City of David II: Imported Stamped Amphora Handles, Coins, Worked Bone and Ivory, and Glass*, vol. 30. Jerusalem: Qedem.

In preparation:

De Groot, A., and D. T. Ariel, eds. *Roman and Byzantine Finds in the City of David and Other Studies*, vol. 3.

Tarler, D., and J. M. Cahill. *Area G*, vol. 4.

De Groot, A. *Area E*, vol. 5.

Naveh, J., and Y. Shoham. *Inscriptions from the City of David*, vol. 6.

De Groot, A., ed. *The Areas Outside the Walls, Part A*, vol. 7.

Gil, D. *The Water Systems of the City of David: Geologic Study, Part B*, vol. 7.